Collins

CW00802174

Reading Comprehension Progress Tests

Year 5/P6

Author:
Stephanie Austwick

Series editors:
Stephanie Austwick
and **Rachel Clarke**

William Collins's dream of knowledge for all began with the publication of his first book in 1819.

A self-educated mill worker, he not only enriched millions of lives, but also founded a flourishing publishing house. Today, staying true to this spirit, Collins books are packed with inspiration, innovation and practical expertise. They place you at the centre of a world of possibility and give you exactly what you need to explore it.

Collins. Freedom to teach.

Published by Collins
An imprint of HarperCollinsPublishers
The News Building
1 London Bridge Street
London
SE1 9GF

> Browse the complete Collins catalogue at
> **www.collins.co.uk**

© HarperCollinsPublishers Limited 2019

10 9 8 7 6 5 4 3 2 1

ISBN 978-0-00-833346-1

British Library Cataloguing-in-Publication Data

A catalogue record for this publication is available from the British Library.

Author: Stephanie Austwick

Series editor: Rachel Clarke

Publisher: Katie Sergeant

Product Manager: Catherine Martin

Development editor: Judith Walters

Copyeditor and typesetter: Hugh Hillyard-Parker

Proofreader: Catherine Dakin

Cover designers: The Big Mountain

Production controller: Katharine Willard

Printed and bound by CPI Group (UK) Ltd, Croydon, CR0 4YY

MIX
Paper from
responsible sources
FSC
www.fsc.org **FSC™ C007454**

The publishers gratefully acknowledge the permission granted to reproduce the copyright material in this book. Every effort has been made to trace copyright holders and to obtain their permission for the use of copyright material. The publishers will gladly receive any information enabling them to rectify any error or omission at the first opportunity.

TEXT

An extract on pp.7-8 from *The Jungle Book* reprinted by permission of HarperCollins Publishers Ltd © 2015 Narinder Dhami; An extract on p.9 from *Code Making, Code Breaking* reprinted by permission of HarperCollins Publishers Ltd © 2011 Richard Platt; An extract on pp.15-16 from *The World's First Women Doctors* by Isabel Thomas reprinted by permission of HarperCollins Publishers Ltd © HarperCollins Publishers Ltd 2015; An extract on p.17 from *Ruby Redfort: Look into My Eyes* reprinted by permission of HarperCollins Publishers Ltd © 2011 Lauren Child; An extract on pp.23-25 from *Jaws and Claws and Things with Wings* reprinted by permission of HarperCollins Publishers Ltd © 2013 Valerie Bloom; An extract on p.34 from *Michael Rosen – All About Me* reprinted by permission of HarperCollins Publishers Ltd © 2009 Michael Rosen; An extract on pp.35-37 from *I Have a Dream* reprinted by permission of HarperCollins Publishers Ltd © 2013 Levi David Addai; An extract on pp.44-45 from *The Boswall Kidnapping* by Keith Gray reprinted by permission of HarperCollins Publishers Ltd © HarperCollins Publishers Ltd 2011; An extract on pp.54-55 from *The Traveller's Guide to the Solar System* reprinted by permission of HarperCollins Publishers Ltd © 2008 Giles Sparrow; An extract on pp.56-57 from *Three Weird Days and a Meteorite* reprinted by permission of HarperCollins Publishers Ltd © 2012 Judy Allen.

IMAGES

p.7 Reprinted by permission of HarperCollins Publishers Ltd © 1999 Piers Sanford; p.9 Claudio Divizia/Shutterstock; p.15t Science History Images/Alamy Stock Photo; p.15b The Picture Art Collection/Alamy Stock Photo; p.17 beboy/Shutterstock; pp.23-24 Illustration by Matt Robertson reprinted by permission of HarperCollins Publishers Ltd © HarperCollins Publishers Ltd 2013; p.25 Illustration by Matt Robertson reprinted by permission of HarperCollins Publishers Ltd © HarperCollins Publishers Ltd 2013; p.26 © HarperCollins Publishers Ltd 2019; p.34 Illustration by Tim Archbold reprinted by permission of HarperCollins Publishers Ltd © HarperCollins Publishers Ltd 2009; p.35 Illustration by Qi Debrah reprinted by permission of HarperCollins Publishers Ltd © HarperCollins Publishers Ltd 2013; p.44 Illustration by Arianna Operamolla reprinted by permission of HarperCollins Publishers Ltd © HarperCollins Publishers Ltd 2011; p.45 Illustration by Arianna Operamolla reprinted by permission of HarperCollins Publishers Ltd © HarperCollins Publishers Ltd 2011; p.46t leosapiens/Shutterstock; p.46b leosapiens/Shutterstock; p.47 YANUSHEVSKAYA VICTORIA/Shutterstock; p.54 Reprinted by permission of HarperCollins Publishers Ltd © 2008 Giles Sparrow; p.56 Illustration by Cherie Zamazing reprinted by permission of HarperCollins Publishers Ltd © HarperCollins Publishers Ltd 2012.

Contents

How to use this book

Introduction

Collins *Reading Comprehension Progress Tests* have been designed to give you a consistent whole-school approach to teaching and assessing reading comprehension. Each photocopiable book covers the required reading comprehension objectives from the 2014 Primary English National Curriculum. For teachers in Scotland, the books can offer guidance and structure that is not provided in the Curriculum for Excellence Experiences and Outcomes or Benchmarks.

As standalone tests, independent of any teaching and learning scheme, the Collins *Reading Comprehension Progress Tests* provide a structured way to assess progress in reading comprehension skills, to help you identify areas for development, and to provide evidence towards expectations for each year group.

Assessment of higher order reading skills

At the end of Key Stage 1 and Key Stage 2, children are assessed on their ability to demonstrate reading comprehension. This is done through national tests (SATs) accompanied by teacher assessment. Collins *Reading Comprehension Progress Tests* have been designed to provide children with opportunities to explore a range of texts whilst building familiarity with the format, language and style of the SATs. Using the tests with your classes each half-term will offer you a snapshot of your pupils' progress throughout the year.

The tests draw on a wide range of text types, from original stories, poems and playscripts, to engaging non-fiction material. The questions follow the style and format of SATs papers at a level appropriate to the year group, and the tests provide increasing challenge within each year group and across the school. Regular use of the progress tests should help children to develop and practise the necessary skills required to complete the national tests with confidence.

How to use this book

In this book, you will find six photocopiable half-termly tests. Each child will need a copy of the test. You will also find a Curriculum Map on page 6 indicating the aspects of the Content Domain covered in each test across the year group. These have been cross-referenced with the appropriate age-related statements from the National Curriculum.

The Year 5 tests demonstrate standard SATs-style questions and mirror the recognised KS2 format of whole texts followed by an answer booklet. Each test includes two contrasting texts. There is no set amount of time for completion of these tests but a guide is to allow approximately one minute per mark. However, the length of text increases in Tests 5 and 6 so it is important to develop children's reading stamina and fluency and teach them how to retrieve information quickly, efficiently and accurately.

To help you mark the tests, you will find mark schemes that include the number of marks to be awarded, model answers and a reference to the elements of the Content Domain covered by each question.

Test demand

The tests have been written to ensure smooth progression in children's reading comprehension within the book and across the rest of the books in the series. Each test builds on those before it so that children are guided towards the expectations of the SATs at the end of KS1 and KS2.

Year group	Test	Number of texts per test	Length of text per test	Number of marks per test
5	Autumn 1	2	Up to 900 words in total	30
5	Autumn 2	2	Up to 900 words in total	30
5	Spring 1	2	Up to 900 words in total	30
5	Spring 2	2	Up to 900 words in total	30
5	Summer 1	2	Up to 1000 words in total	30
5	Summer 2	2	Up to 1000 words in total	30

Performance thresholds

The table below provides guidance for assessing how children perform in the tests. Most children should achieve scores at or above the expected standard with some children working at greater depth and exceeding expectations for their year group. Whilst these threshold bands do not represent standardised scores, as in the end of key stage SATs, they will give an indication of how pupils are performing against the expected standard for their year group.

Year group	Test	Working towards	Expected	Greater depth
5	Autumn 1	15 marks or below	16–23 marks	24–30 marks
5	Autumn 2	15 marks or below	16–23 marks	24–30 marks
5	Spring 1	15 marks or below	16–23 marks	24–30 marks
5	Spring 2	15 marks or below	16–23 marks	24–30 marks
5	Summer 1	15 marks or below	16–23 marks	24–30 marks
5	Summer 2	15 marks or below	16–23 marks	24–30 marks

Tracking progress

A record sheet is provided to help you illustrate to children the areas in which their reading comprehension is strong and where they need to develop. A spreadsheet tracker is also provided via **collins.co.uk/assessment/downloads** which enables you to identify whole-class patterns of attainment. This can be used to inform your next teaching and learning steps.

Editable download

All the files are available online in Word and PDF format. Go to **collins.co.uk/assessment/downloads** to find instructions on how to download. The files are password protected and the password clue is included on the website. You will need to use the clue to locate the password in your book.

You can use the editable Word files to help you meet the specific needs of your class, whether that be by increasing or decreasing the challenge, by reducing the amount of questions, by providing more space for answers or increasing the size of text as required for specific children.

Year 5 Curriculum map: Yearly overview

National Curriculum objective (Year 5)	Content domain	Test 1		Test 2			Test 3		Test 4		Test 5		Test 6	
		Fiction	Non-fiction	Non-fiction	Fiction	Poetry	Non-fiction	Non-fiction	Non-fiction	Play-script	Fiction	Poetry	Non-fiction	Fiction
Identify and discuss themes and conventions in and across writing.	2f Identify/explain how information/narrative content is related and contributes to meaning as a whole.										●	●		●
Make comparisons within and across texts.	2h Make comparisons within the text.		●			●					●	●		●
Discuss the meaning of words in context.	2a Give/explain the meaning of words in context.	●	●	●	●	●	●		●	●		●	●	●
Draw inferences such as inferring characters' feelings, thoughts and motives from their actions, and justifying inferences with evidence.	2d Make inferences from the text / explain and justify inferences with evidence from the text	●	●	●	●	●	●		●	●	●		●	●
Predict what might happen from details stated and implied.	2e Predict what might happen from details stated and implied.													
Summarise the main ideas drawn from more than one paragraph (or verse) identifying key details that support the main ideas.	2c Summarise main ideas from more than one paragraph.	●	●	●	●		●		●	●	●	●		
Identify how language, structure and presentation contribute to meaning.	2g Identify/explain how meaning is enhanced through choice of words and phrases.					●							●	
Discuss and evaluate how authors use language, including figurative language, considering the impact on the reader.	2g Identify/explain how meaning is enhanced through choice of words and phrases.					●					●		●	
Distinguish between statements of fact and opinion.	2d Make inferences from the text / explain and justify inferences with evidence from the text.	●	●	●	●	●	●		●	●	●		●	
Retrieve and record information/identify key details from fiction and non-fiction text.	2b Retrieve and record information / identify key details from fiction and non-fiction.	●	●	●	●	●	●		●	●	●	●	●	●
Provide reasoned justification to support views.	2d Make inferences from the text / explain and justify inferences with evidence from the text.	●	●	●	●	●	●		●	●	●	●	●	●

From *The Jungle Book*

written by Rudyard Kipling, retold by Narinder Dhami

"Mowgli the Jungle Boy!"

The village children chased me down the street, calling me names. "Wolf Man!"

"Go away!" I shouted at them. "Just leaf me alone!"

They all burst out laughing. "You mean 'leave', not 'leaf'!" one of the boys sneered. "You can't even speak properly!"

Three months had passed since I'd come to the village, and every day I wished I was back in the jungle. I was still learning the human's language, and I kept getting words wrong, although Messua tried to teach me. I didn't understand the children's games, so I couldn't join in with them. Anyway, they just called me names and ran away from me.

I didn't understand their human laws, either. Why did the village people wear so many clothes, and what was the point of money? Why did the poor people work so hard, whilst the rich people did nothing?

Messua was very kind to me, but I longed to go back to my real home in the jungle.

Every night, the head of the village and all the men would meet under the great fig tree to tell the jungle tales. I soon realised they didn't know what they were talking about! Once I heard one of them telling a story about the ghost-tiger who'd stolen Messua's baby son.

I couldn't help laughing.

"Shere Khan's no ghost-tiger," I said. "All your jungle stories are lies!"

The head man was very annoyed. "Tomorrow you'll do something useful and start herding the village cattle!" he snapped.

So every day, riding on the back of Rama the great bull, I took the cattle and the buffaloes out to the plains to graze. I lay under the trees while the cattle ate the grass and the buffaloes wallowed in the pools.

I never forgot to check the tall rock. Every day one of my wolf brothers was there. But then, one day, there was no one on top of the rock.

Now I knew Shere Khan had returned, and that this time either he or I had to die.

Immediately, I leapt onto Rama's back and drove the cattle and the buffaloes across the plain. When we arrived at the tall rock, Grey Brother sprang out of a clump of bamboo.

"Shere Khan's back?" I asked, my heart pounding inside me. But I already knew the answer.

Grey Brother nodded.

"He's hiding close by, in a deep, narrow valley on the other side of the plain," he replied. "He'll come for you at nightfall."

From *Code Making, Code Breaking*

by Richard Platt

What are codes and secret languages?

If you think only spies and soldiers use codes, you're wrong! We all use codes. They help us to address letters, talk on a phone, or even choose clothes.

Not all codes are secret. Some are easy ways to pass on facts quickly.

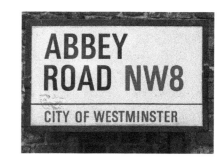

For example, a postcode describes your street in six or seven letters and numbers. Anybody can find out what this code means. Secret codes are different. They have the opposite aim. They hide the meaning of a message. Secret codes are also called ciphers. Once a message is encoded (written in secret code), only someone who understands the code can read it.

Spies and soldiers have used secret codes to hide their plans almost since warfare began. But secret codes also keep all sorts of everyday things private. They hide your identity on the internet and they even stop people listening in to your mobile phone calls.

Ancient messages: smoke and fire

When a Greek army went to war around 3,200 years ago, it used a code to send news home. Mountaintop bonfires carried its message 600 kilometres. The flames signalled 'victory', which meant 'We beat the Trojans!'

Fires carry news fast. We see their bright glow by night and their smoke by day. However, fires send only simple signals: a lit fire could mean 'victory' or 'yes', and an unlit fire could mean 'defeat' or 'no'.

Native American people used smoke for smarter messages. The Apache built three fires to signal 'alarm!'. Their families could see the three smoke plumes up to 80 kilometres away. Two fires signalled 'We have made a camp.' Just one meant 'attention!'.

In 1775, Americans fighting the British signalled with lantern flames. Their code was one light if troops advanced by land and two if they arrived by sea.

Name:	Class:	Date:

> Questions 1–10 are about *The Jungle Book*
> (pages 7–8).

1 Which **two** statements are correct?

✓ Tick **two**.

The village children were unkind to Mowgli. ☐

Mowgli was a wolf. ☐

Mowgli couldn't speak. ☐

Mowgli was learning a new language. ☐

1 mark

2 Why did Mowgli find it hard to play with the other children?
Give **two** reasons, using evidence from the text

1. _____

2. _____

2 marks

3 Why do you think Mowgli didn't understand the *human laws* in the village? Support your answer with reference to **two** of the laws in the text.

_____

_____

_____

_____

2 marks

4 What was Mowgli's opinion of the jungle tales told by the village men?

_____

1 mark

5 *I took the cattle and the buffaloes out to the plains to graze.*

What do you think is meant by the word *graze*?

_____

1 mark

6 How do you think Mowgli felt when he noticed that the top of the tall rock was empty, and why?

_____

_____

_____

2 marks

7 What type of animal was Grey Brother?

_____

1 mark

8 Put ticks (✓) in the table to show which of these statements are **true** and which are **false**.

	True	False
Shere Khan was dangerous.		
Mowgli's friend was hiding in the bamboo.		
Shere Khan had been away.		
Grey Brother would meet Mowgli at nightfall.		

2 marks

9   Why do you think Mowgli's heart was *pounding* in his chest?

_____

_____

1 mark

10   Using evidence from the whole text, what do you predict might happen at nightfall?

_____

_____

_____

_____

2 marks

Questions 11–20 are about *Code Making, Code Breaking* (page 9).

11   According to the text, who uses codes?

_____

1 mark

12   Explain the meaning of:

a) *cipher*   _____

b) *encoded*   _____

2 marks

13 Draw **four** lines to match the people to their method of signalling in times of war.

Greek army	smoke
Native Americans	a code using three plumes of smoke
Americans fighting the British	mountaintop bonfires
The Apache	lantern flames

2 marks

14 Which was better – using one fire or three fires? Why?

_____

_____

2 marks

15 According to the text, what different meanings did one lantern and two lanterns have?

_____

_____

_____

2 marks

16 **Find** and **copy** the word from the text that means *a win*.

_____

1 mark

17 Put ticks (✓) in the table to show which of these might be used **in the home today** and which by **armies in the past**.

Some may appear in both columns.

	In the home today	Armies in the past
a computer password		
smoke		
a mobile phone lock code		
a lantern		
a postcode		
a secret code		

2 marks

18 This extract is from a text called *Code Making, Code Breaking*.
Explain the term *code breaking*.

_____

1 mark

19 Why might it be important for an army to break a code?

_____

_____

1 mark

20 Have you ever used a code mentioned in the text? Explain when and why you used it.

_____

_____

1 mark

From *The World's First Women Doctors*

by Isabel Thomas

How to build a pioneer

In the early 1800s, the 'normal' path for middle-class girls was to get married and have children. Work was seen as unladylike. Luckily, Elizabeth Blackwell and Elizabeth Garrett Anderson were born into families that weren't afraid to do things differently.

Meet the Blackwells

Elizabeth Blackwell was born in Bristol, England, in 1821. Her family moved to the USA when she was 11. Samuel Blackwell, Elizabeth's father, always tried to do the right thing, even if it made him unpopular. He didn't allow his daughters to do frivolous things such as wear pretty clothes or learn how to sew. Instead, they grew up meeting interesting people and campaigning against slavery.

Meet the Garretts

Elizabeth Garrett Anderson was born in 1836, and grew up near the seaside in Suffolk, England. Her father, Newson Garrett, wanted to give his sons and his daughters a good education. Garrett Anderson spent two years at boarding school and kept studying after she left. By the time she was 16, Elizabeth knew that she wanted to work for a living.

Feeling trapped

As teenagers, both Elizabeth Blackwell and Elizabeth Garrett Anderson began to worry about the next stage of their lives. They didn't feel excited about the 'normal' path ahead.

The expected paths in the 1800s

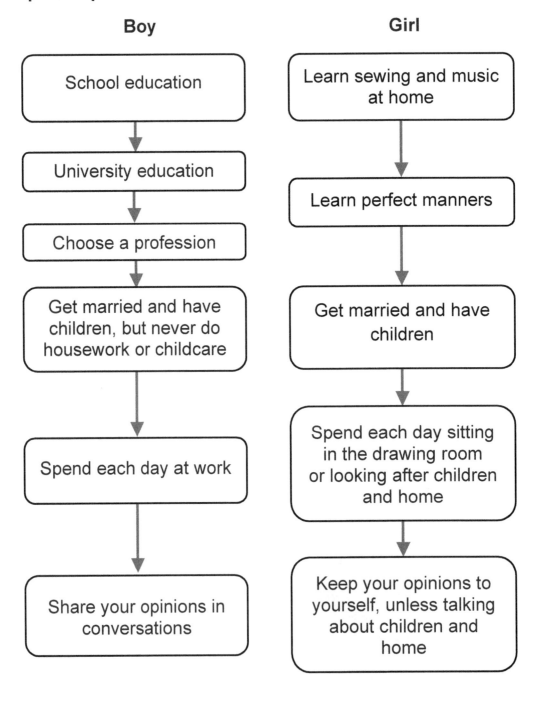

Boy

School education
↓
University education
↓
Choose a profession
↓
Get married and have children, but never do housework or childcare
↓
Spend each day at work
↓
Share your opinions in conversations

Girl

Learn sewing and music at home
↓
Learn perfect manners
↓
Get married and have children
↓
Spend each day sitting in the drawing room or looking after children and home
↓
Keep your opinions to yourself, unless talking about children and home

From *Ruby Redfort: Look into My Eyes*

by Lauren Child

Ruby Redfort was perched on a high stool in front of the bathroom window, her binoculars trained on a cake delivery truck that had been parked on Cedarwood Drive for precisely 21 minutes.

So far no one had emerged from the truck with so much as a blueberry muffin. Ruby gurgled down the last dregs of her banana milk and made a note in the little yellow notebook which lay in her lap. She had 622 of these yellow notebooks; all but one was stashed under her bedroom floorboards. Though she had taken up this hobby nine years ago, no one, not even her best friend Clancy, had read a single word she had written. Much of what Ruby observed seemed pretty mundane but EVEN THE MUNDANE CAN TELL A STORY {RULE 16}.

Ruby also kept a vivid pink notebook, dog-eared and smelling of bubble gum, and it was in this that she listed her Ruby rules – there were 79 so far.

RULE 1: YOU CAN NEVER BE COMPLETELY SURE WHAT MIGHT HAPPEN NEXT. A truth no one could argue with.

Ruby was a petite girl, small for her years – at first glance a very ordinary looking kid. There was nothing particular to mark her out – that is, nothing until you looked a little longer. Then you would begin to see that her eyes were ever so slightly different shades of green. When they looked at you, it was somehow hard to remember the point you were arguing. And when she smiled, she revealed small doll-like teeth which somehow made it impossible to consider her anything other than a cute kid. But the most striking thing about Ruby Redfort was that when you met her you felt a strong need for her to like you. The bathroom phone rang; lazily, Ruby reached out and groped for the receiver.

'Brandy's wig salon, hair today, gone tomorrow.'

'Hi Rube,' came back the voice on the other end; it was Clancy Crew.

'So Clance, what gives?'

'Not a whole lot actually.'

'So to what do I owe the pleasure of this call?'

'Boredom,' yawned Clancy.

'So why don't you get yourself over here, bozo?'

'Well, I would you know Rube but my dad wants me home – he's got some kinda embassy type function and he wants us all smiling, you know what I mean?'

Name:	Class:	Date:

> Questions 1–10 are about *The World's First Women Doctors* (pages 15–16).

1 Which word is used in the text to describe *work* in the early 1800s?

✓ Tick **one**.

normal ☐

middle class ☐

unladylike ☐

different ☐

_____

1 mark

2 **Find** and **copy** the names of the **two** women who were *born into families that weren't afraid to do things differently*.

1. _____

2. _____

_____

2 marks

3 When and where was Elizabeth Blackwell born?

_____

_____

1 mark

4 Elizabeth's father *always tried to do the right thing, even if it made him unpopular*.

Explain the meaning of the word *unpopular* in this sentence.

_____

_____

1 mark

5 What **two** things did Elizabeth Blackwell do instead of learning how to sew?

1. _____

2. _____

2 marks

6 Put ticks (✔) in the table to show which of these are **true** and which are **false**.

	True	False
Elizabeth Garrett Anderson spent her childhood in Suffolk.		
Elizabeth Blackwell was born in the USA.		
Elizabeth Blackwell was born before Elizabeth Garrett Anderson.		
Garrett Anderson went to boarding school.		

1 mark

7 What did Newson Garrett want his sons *and* his daughters to have, and why do you think he might have felt it was important?

_____

_____

2 marks

8 How did both girls feel about the *'normal' path ahead* and why? Support you answers with evidence from the **whole** text.

_____

_____

_____

2 marks

9   Put ticks (✓) in the table to show which of these are **fact** and which are **opinion**.

	Fact	Opinion
Elizabeth Garrett Anderson had brothers and sisters.		
Wearing pretty clothes is frivolous.		
Boarding schools provide the best education.		
Girls in the 1800s were expected to get married and have children.		

2 marks

10   Girls were told: *keep your opinions to yourself.*

Explain the meaning of this instruction.

_____

_____

1 mark

Questions 11–20 are about ***Ruby Redfort: Look into My Eyes***
(page 17).

---

11   According to the text, where **exactly** was Ruby?

_____

1 mark

12   *So far no one had emerged from the truck.*

Circle the word that has a similar meaning to the word *emerged*.

called   waved   appeared   hidden

1 mark

13 How do you think Ruby felt about her yellow notebooks? Give **two** reasons for your answer, using evidence from the text.

1. _____

_____

2. _____

_____

2 marks

14 Number the sentences below from **1** to **4** to show the order of events.

Ruby drank her banana milk. ☐

The telephone rang. ☐

A truck pulled up in Cedarwood Drive. ☐

Ruby made a note in her notebook. ☐

2 marks

15 Why do you think Ruby was watching the truck so intently? Support your answer with evidence from the text.

_____

_____

_____

2 marks

16 How does the author describe Ruby's eyes?

_____

_____

1 mark

17 *But the most striking thing about Ruby Redfort was that when you met her you felt a strong need for her to like you.*

Explain the work *striking* in this context.

_____

1 mark

18 Ruby has a sense of humour. How has the author shown this?

_____

_____

_____

_____

2 marks

19 Why couldn't Clancy come over to Ruby's house?

_____

1 mark

20 What is your impression of Ruby Redfort's personality?

Support you answer with evidence from the **whole** text.

_____

_____

_____

2 marks

From *Jaws and Claws and Things with Wings*

by Valerie Bloom

Whale Alert

Teacher said, "Research an animal, in the sea, the air, the ground,"
I chose to find out about the whale and this is what I found.

The whale is peaceful, the whale is smart,
The whale's got a song that could melt your heart.

Whales can't taste, and whales can't smell,
But whales can hear extremely well.

A whale that's singing – folk who know whales say –
Can be heard by others a hundred miles away.

A whale talks with a whistle, a squeak or a click,
Though he's big as a mountain, a whale's very quick.

They have no teeth, so they cannot chew,
And live on fishy things smaller'n me and you.

They never hurt people, so I'm sad to know
That people could treat the poor whale so.

They hunt him for his meat, for his oil and bone,
They will not leave the whale alone.

In just 50 years, two million have died,
Each with a harpoon growing from its side.

One day, there may be no more whales,
Except those living in fairy tales.

Fairy tales are good places for fairy folk to be,
But whales would be happier living in the sea.

The Lion Lay Still in the Zoo

The lion lay still in the zoo,
And dreamt of forests and streams.
The cage was sparkling and new,
The lion lay still in the zoo.
The people who crowded his view,
Tried to rouse him with shouts and with screams,
But the lion lay still in the zoo,
And dreamt of forests and streams.

Step Back, Step Forward

by Stephanie Austwick

Plastic is a remarkable and versatile product – but it is polluting our planet!

Take a moment to look around you. It's everywhere! It's hard to live without it. Or is it?

In the past, people managed to do just that, so why not now?

Prior to the 1960s, there was no plastic pollution … anywhere. It wasn't because plastic didn't exist – in fact, plastic had actually been invented in the early 19th century.

However, by the end of the 1950s, the manufacturing of plastics had become easier. Combined with an abundance of oil – which is needed to make plastic – the mass production of cheap disposable plastic products began, and it is these single-use products that are destroying the planet.

Just think about the things you throw away when you have finished using them – bottles, bags, food wrappers, packaging, pens, toys … the list goes on.

But it wasn't always like this. Let's take a trip down memory lane and see what we can learn from the past.

Milk was delivered to the door in glass bottles, which were then collected, washed and used again … and again. On average, a milk bottle was reused 50 times! Some people are lucky enough to still have this service.

Water came from the tap, but soft drinks also came in glass bottles, with the added incentive of a reward – money back for each bottle returned. Children kept their eagle eyes open for any that might be lying around!

Homes did not have fridges so, several times a week, the person in charge of the cooking, usually the housewife or housekeeper, would take a wicker basket and set off to the local shops in search of something fresh and tasty.

First stop might be the butcher's, where a cut of meat would be selected from one of the many carcasses hanging up on giant metal hooks. The butcher would slice the required amount and wrap it in paper to be placed in the basket.

Next, to the greengrocer's to choose from the limited selection of fresh fruit and vegetables currently in season. The shop assistant would weigh the produce, which would then be placed in the basket, alongside the meat. Fruit or vegetables that were not in season could be purchased in tin cans.

After that, the grocer's might be next on the list. Huge hessian sacks of dried goods – such as sugar, flour, rice and dried fruit – and wooden chests of loose tea leaves were lined up on the floor. The grocer would use a shiny metal scoop to transfer the goods to the scales and, once weighed, they would be tipped into brown paper or sugar-paper bags and folded tight.

Glistening slabs of butter and cheese would be sliced, weighed and wrapped in greaseproof paper before being transferred to the basket.

Finally, to the baker's for a freshly-baked loaf, which would also be wrapped in fine tissue paper and placed on the top.

Not a plastic bag, bottle or package in sight!

Although we may not wish to return to those days, the need to reduce our reliance on unnecessary plastic packaging is an urgent one. Many of us have already invested in 'bags for life' or refillable water bottles, but this is just the start.

Our planet is suffocating under a blanket of plastic.

What could you do to help?

| Name: | Class: | Date: |

Questions 1–9 are about *Jaws and Claws and Things with Wings* (pages 23–25).

Read '**Whale Alert**'.

1 *Research an animal, in the sea, the air, the ground.*

Tick two words that have a similar meaning to *research*.

✓ Tick **two**.

make ☐

study ☐

watch ☐

investigate ☐

1 mark

2 Find and copy **two** adjectives used to describe the whale.

1. _____

2. _____

1 mark

3 *The whale's got a song that could melt your heart.*

Explain the meaning of this phrase.

_____

_____

1 mark

4 How far does the song of a whale travel?

_____

1 mark

5 According to the text, **a) how** and **b) why** do people kill whales?

a) _____

b) _____

2 marks

Read '**The Lion Lay Still in the Zoo**'.

6 What was the lion dreaming about in this poem?

_____

1 mark

7 Do you think the lion was happy? Support your answer with evidence from the text.

_____

_____

_____

2 marks

8 *The people who crowded his view,*
Tried to rouse him with shouts and with screams.

Circle the word that has a similar meaning to *rouse*.

annoy   awaken   frighten   upset

1 mark

Read '**Whale Alert**' *and* '**The Lion Lay Still in the Zoo**'.

9 From the way the poet has written these poems, what impression do you get of her attitude towards these creatures?

Support your answers with reference to the text.

_____

_____

_____

_____

2 marks

Questions 10–20 are about '**Step Back, Step Forward**'
(pages 26–27).

10 According to the text, what is plastic doing to our planet?

_____

1 mark

11 **Find** and **copy** the word in the text that means the same as 'before'.

_____

1 mark

12 Explain the phrase *mass-produced disposable plastic products*.

_____

_____

2 marks

13 Put ticks (✓) in the table to show which of these are **true** and which are **false**.

	True	False
Soft drinks came in glass bottles.		
Milk bottles could be reused five times.		
It is still possible to have milk delivered.		
Water bottles were also made of glass.		

2 marks

14 Why do you think *Children kept their eagle eyes open*?

_____

_____

2 marks

15 *to choose from the limited selection of fresh fruit and vegetables.*

Underline **one** word that has a similar meaning to the word *limited*.

restricted   good   interesting   unusual

1 mark

16 List **four** items that might be displayed in sacks, according to the text.

_____

1 mark

17 Draw **four** lines to match the item to the shop.

butter	butcher's
carrots and potatoes	baker's
bread	grocer's
beef and lamb	greengrocer's

1 mark

18 Why do you think people had to shop several times a week?

_____

_____

2 marks

19 Put ticks (✔) in the table to show which of these are **fact** and which are **opinion**.

	Fact	Opinion
Plastic is a remarkable product.		
Oil is needed to make plastic.		
You are lucky if you still have a milkman.		
People did not used to buy bottled water.		

2 marks

20 In the past, people lived without disposable plastic.

With reference to the text, summarise **three** ways they managed to do this.

_____

_____

_____

_____

_____

3 marks

From *Michael Rosen: All About Me* (An autobiography)

by Michael Rosen

When I was 11, I took an exam called the 11-plus. This decided whether you should go to the grammar school or a secondary modern school.

The whole of my last two years at primary school, which are now called Years Five and Six, were full of worry about whether we would pass this exam or not.

Every week we did tests, an English test and a Maths test, and our teacher would average up the marks and put us in a place in the class according to the mark. So that meant every week we changed where we sat in the class. Now that in itself didn't matter too much: you just took your stuff out of your desk and moved. But you didn't get a chance to sit with your friends or at a table you liked. I always wanted to sit in twelfth place because the person who was twelfth always got to ring the school bell. I was never twelfth though.

I remember the day the results came, and seeing the envelope on the doormat in our flat. I didn't want to open it because I was so worried that I wouldn't pass.

I did pass though, and on the way to school, everyone was calling to each other across the park, "Did you pass? Did you pass?"

The next school I went to was a mixed grammar school for people who had passed that 11-plus exam. It was halfway up a big hill called Harrow Weald, surrounded by oak trees.

We weren't allowed in through the front door.

I hung about in a group of boys who were all very, very funny. We loved messing around doing accents, and we used to spend hours in our breaks imitating teachers, or pretending to be people on the television or in films.

From *I Have a Dream*

by Levi David Addai

TERESA: So this is all some sort of joke to you?

RAHEEM: No, Mum.

TERESA: I've never been so embarrassed. Did you even think how your actions might reflect on me? How can I be teaching other children when I can't control my own? It's embarrassing! And what was the meaning of this?

RAHEEM: It was just some Black History project.

TERESA: An important History project! All you had to do was write your own "I have a dream" speech but what did you do, Raheem? What type of nonsense is this?

RAHEEM: But Mum, they're not all bad. I did write about other more ... serious dreams.

TERESA: What, like the dream about (*looking at essay*) "time-travelling" or the dream of being "rich and famous"?

RAHEEM: But I do wanna be rich and famous. (*Teresa sighs.*)

TERESA: You know what? You can go to your room – I haven't got the patience for this right now.

RAHEEM: If I was Reece Smith or Ryan Collins, you wouldn't be coming heavy like this, but because I'm Raheem Harris, son of Ms Harris, teacher of 4A, I get it worst.

TERESA: Do you even care about your future?

RAHEEM: Yeah, of course.

TERESA: Because all I've heard today is how you muck around and won't do what Miss Wallace asks. (*waving Raheem's exercise book*) And as for this, this should have been easy! I should be hearing that you got an A star or something!

RAHEEM: What? 'Cos it was about Martin Luther King? I'm fed up of hearing about that guy, man.

TERESA: Why?

RAHEEM: 'Cos he got shot dead! He's got nothing to do with my life or anything.

TERESA: But look how many stories I've told you about him. I've shown you how his work helped bring change to the world.

RAHEEM: Yeah, his world in the stone-aged years. It's useless. What's the point of learning about it?

TERESA: (*horrified*) What's the point?

RAHEEM: I can't be bothered with that, man. It's boring; he's boring.

TERESA: Do you know what my dream was, when I was your age?

RAHEEM: I bet it was to do with something boring, like being a teacher.

TERESA: You're right, it was.

RAHEEM: I knew it!

TERESA: But I got there, didn't I? And you know how?

RAHEEM: Nope.

TERESA: Through hard work.

RAHEEM: I don't wanna be a teacher.

TERESA: I didn't say you have to be. I'm just curious to know what your dream is Raheem. It might help you ... focus more.

RAHEEM: Well, I gave an answer, but you ruled it out so I guess I don't have one.

TERESA: But you see, if you don't have a dream, how you gonna have a dream come true?

RAHEEM: What am I – five? Gosh! Life ain't like a Disney film, man. Dreams don't come true. They're just ... dreams.

TERESA: Oh really?

RAHEEM: And you being a teacher doesn't count.

TERESA: OK, Mr Cynical. But, what if I was to tell you that my new dream is to become the head teacher at your school?

RAHEEM: Huh? Are you serious? You can't do that!

TERESA: Why not? It's my dream.

RAHEEM: But ... but ... what about me?

TERESA: I've been a teacher at your school for how many years now and you've been fine. Nothing's going to change.

RAHEEM: It will! This is so unfair!

TERESA: No, what would be unfair would be me not being able to apply for the job in the first place.

RAHEEM: Why would they stop you?

TERESA: Because there was a time when people that looked like you and me weren't allowed to do certain things, at least not with everyone else. But people like Martin Luther King fought hard so that I could be treated the same.

RAHEEM: Here we go again.

Name:	Class:	Date:

> Questions 1–9 are about **Michael Rosen: All About Me** (page 34).

1 What was the name of the exam Michael took when he was 11?

_____

1 mark

2 Using the text, complete this sentence:

The whole of my last two years at primary school were …

✓ Tick **one**.

spent at a grammar school ☐

spent at a secondary modern school ☐

full of worry ☐

were called Years Five and Six ☐

1 mark

3 Name **two** things that happened every week in Michael's class.

1. _____

_____

2. _____

_____

2 marks

4 Why did Michael want to come twelfth in the tests?

_____

1 mark

5 Find the word *results*. Circle the word that has a similar meaning.

post   rewards   outcomes   insults

_____
1 mark

6 Number the sentences below from **1** to **4** to show the order in which they happened.

Michael went to grammar school.   ☐

The results arrived.   ☐

Michael took the 11-plus exam.   ☐

Friends asked him if he'd passed.   ☐

_____
1 mark

7 How do you think Michael felt **before** and **after** he opened the envelope containing his results? Support your answer with evidence from the text.

_____

_____

_____

_____

_____
2 marks

8 According to the text, what did Michael and his friends do at break times? Explain what this might mean.

_____

_____

_____

_____
2 marks

9 This is an extract from an *autobiography*.

Explain the meaning of this term.

_____

_____

1 mark

Questions 10–20 are about *I Have a Dream* (pages 35–37).

10 This play is about two characters. What is their relationship?

_____

1 mark

11 Tick the sentence which summarises the action in the opening of this scene.

✓ Tick **one**.

Teresa was listening to Raheem's jokes. ☐

Raheem wanted to be rich and famous. ☐

Teresa was confronting Raheem about his attitude. ☐

Raheem was sent to his room. ☐

1 mark

12 *Teresa: (horrified) What's the point?*

Give **two** adjectives with a similar meaning to *horrified* that the playwright could have used as stage directions.

_____   _____

2 marks

13 This play script is written using an informal style.

　　a) Give an example of this from the text.
　　b) Explain why you think the author has written in this way.

　　a) _____

　　b) _____

　　　_____

2 marks

14 Put ticks (✓) in the table to show which of these are **true** and which are **false**.

	True	False
Miss Wallace is Raheem's teacher.		
Teresa is a teacher at Raheem's school.		
Raheem got an A star for his work.		
Teresa dreamed of being a teacher when she was young.		

2 marks

15 *It might help you … focus more.*

Explain what Teresa means by *focus more.*

_____

1 mark

16 How do you think Raheem feels about his mother applying for the job of head teacher at his school and why? Justify your answer with evidence from the text.

_____

_____

_____

2 marks

17 Raheem compares himself with Reece Smith and Ryan Collins. How did he feel his situation was different?

_____

_____

1 mark

18 Put ticks (✓) in the table to show which of these are **fact** and which are **opinion**.

	Fact	Opinion
Martin Luther King was shot dead.		
It is a good thing to be rich and famous.		
Martin Luther King helped to change the lives of black people.		
It is boring learning about Martin Luther King.		

2 marks

19 How do you think Teresa is feeling during this whole scene?
Support your answer with evidence from the text.

_____

_____

_____

_____

2 marks

20 Do you think Teresa and Raheem have discussed Martin Luther King before?

Give **two** quotations from the text that illustrate this.

_____

_____

_____

_____

2 marks

From *The Boswall Kidnapping*

by Keith Gray

I saw a boy of about my age on the escalator, heading up to the next floor. He had blond hair and was wearing sensible trousers, like school trousers, and a tee shirt that had come untucked. But the weird thing was, even though he had his back to me, I could tell he was crying. Maybe it was the way he was standing, all head-down and saggy shoulders.

None of the other customers seemed to notice him, or even care that he was crying.

I looked for Dad, but he'd wandered off towards a display of tinkly lampshades and wasn't paying any attention to me. So I followed the boy.

I ran up the escalator's moving steps. It felt so important to me to find out what was wrong with this boy.

The first floor is the furniture department. There are lots of tables and beds and wardrobes. A few shoppers were testing out the sofas, but I couldn't see the boy anywhere. I made a guess, thinking he wouldn't want to hang around all this boring stuff and had probably gone through to look at the TVs and radios. That's where I'd go.

But I spotted him walking in the opposite direction. He stopped and looked back over his shoulder. And the way he did it made me look back over my shoulder too.

Not that I could see anything special – just armchairs and stuff.

When I turned back, he'd gone again.

I had to run again. But he hadn't gone far. This department was all kitchen things like kettles and toasters and washing machines. Not what you'd call exciting. I didn't know why he'd want to be in here. But he seemed to be wandering around without looking at anything on the shelves. Half the time he looked at his feet.

I went up behind him and tapped him on the shoulder. He yelped and jumped about two metres in the air.

I laughed. I couldn't help it. "Sorry. I didn't mean –"

"What?" he said. "What?"

"I didn't mean, you know ...? To scare you."

He looked confused and embarrassed. Close up, I reckoned he was a year or two younger than me. He was a centimetre or two shorter than me, as well.

"Leave me alone."

"Honestly, I'm sorry," I said. "I just saw you, and saw you were crying." He scowled at me.

"So?" Then he stared at his feet again. "I'm allowed to cry, aren't I? And anyway, I'm not anymore."

"Yes, you are."

He turned to hide his face, and I felt bad for embarrassing him so much.

"I'm sorry," I said again. "I just wondered why you were ... I thought I could help." I wasn't sure if that was true or not. But I couldn't help feeling curious about why he was crying.

"What do you care anyway?" he said.

I shrugged. "My name's Alex," I told him instead.

He pushed his floppy blond fringe out of his eyes and tried to wipe away some tears. "I'm Sam. And I don't care what you say, or if you think it's stupid to cry. I've lost my mum."

For a second I thought, "Is that all?" I didn't say it out loud, but he must have seen it on my face because he started sniffling again. And I felt mean. He was only young, seemed a bit wimpy too, and maybe he didn't know his way around Boswall's as well as I did.

"I'll help you find her," I said. "Come on, where did you last see her?"

He looked at me like I was mad.

House Speak

by Stephanie Austwick

I miss my old house.

It was warm.

It had a friendly face and walls that welcomed you.

A door that opened and said,

"Come in. Make yourself at home.

Bring your friends."

It had threadbare carpets, squishy sofas,

A lawn with goalposts and no grass,

And windows that winked.

I don't like my new house.

It's cold.

It has a sour expression.

It peers, suspiciously, through narrow windows.

With shiny floors and white walls,

An ugly odour of fresh paint,

And a door that snaps shut behind you,

Shouting "Keep out!"

My friend Al's house is amazing!

It's cool.

It's got a pool!

There are *two* sets of stairs that race each other to the top,

And under-floor heating that tickles
your toes when you take off your shoes,

Which you have to in Al's house.

It's one of the rules.

"Be tidy. Be clean. Behave!" it warns,
the moment you step inside.

He's even got his own shower.

Leah's house is not a house.

It's way up high.

It guards, like a sentry, as you play in the park,

Straight-backed and alert.

And calls to you from the clouds.

"Come on up, the view's fantastic."

So we press the button – and we're never disappointed.

The house in the woods is different.

It's empty.

They call it a ruin, but that can't be right

Because ruined means spoiled

And it's definitely not!

It's a castle, a den, a spaceship, a fort,

An adventure, a story, a land far away.

"Come and play," it beckons, with a mischievous glint.

So we do – wouldn't you?

My Great Gran's house is a cottage, with a greying thatch on top.

It's old.

Like her.

It stoops and it leans, sighing quietly.

The windows are tired; they can hardly keep awake.

But they flutter and blink as I open the gate.

The doors creak, the floorboards squeak

And the pipes gurgle and grumble and rumble.

"Come in, settle down, keep safe," it whispers,

"Play a game; read a story; sing a song; snuggle up."

This house wraps you in love … and chocolate.

Name:	Class:	Date:

Questions 1–10 are about *The Boswall Kidnapping* (pages 44–45).

1 How does the narrator describe the trousers worn by the boy?

✓ Tick **two**.

grey ☐

like school trousers ☐

sensible ☐

smart ☐

1 mark

2 How did Alex know that the boy was crying?

_____

_____

1 mark

3 Alex obviously thought the boy was acting strangely when he was following him. What was he doing?

Support your answer with evidence from the text.

_____

_____

_____

2 marks

4 Why do you think the boy *yelped and jumped about two metres in the air* when Alex tapped him on the shoulder?

_____

1 mark

5 **Find** and **copy two** words from the text that show how the boy was feeling when Alex started to speak to him.

_____   _____

2 marks

6 What reason did the boy give for being upset?

_____

1 mark

7 According to the text, how did Alex feel when the boy *started sniffling again* and why did he feel like this?

_____

_____

_____

2 marks

8 Number the sentences below from **1** to **4** to show the order of events in Boswall's.

The boy entered the furniture department.   ☐

The boy was crying on the escalator.   ☐

Alex followed him into the kitchen department.   ☐

Alex was shopping with his father.   ☐

1 mark

9 Using the **whole** text, give a complete summary of the boy's appearance.

_____

_____

_____

_____

2 marks

10 Using clues from the text, what do you predict *might* happen next?

_____

_____

1 mark

Questions 11–20 are about **'House Speak'** (pages 46–47).

11 Which statement is the best summary of the **whole** of this poem?

✓ Tick **one**.

This poem is about a child's house. ☐

This is a rhyming poem. ☐

This poem describes a number of different houses. ☐

This poem is about someone's favourite houses. ☐

1 mark

12 Read the first two verses. How do the old and new house compare, and which one does the narrator prefer?

_____

_____

_____

_____

2 marks

13 The new house is described as *cold*.

Apart from the temperature, what could this mean?

Circle the word that gives an alternative meaning.

damp   unwelcoming   dark   eerie

1 mark

14 In the verse about Al's house, why do you think the word *two* is in italics?

_____

_____

1 mark

15 *Leah's house is not a house.*

Where do you think Leah lives?

Support your answer with evidence from the text.

_____

_____

2 marks

16 Why does the narrator think it is wrong to call the house in the woods *a ruin*?

_____

_____

2 marks

17 Give **three** ways in which Great Gran's cottage resembles her.

_____   _____   _____

1 mark

18 Put ticks (✔) in the table to show which of these are **true** and which are **false**.

	True	False
You can see for miles from Leah's house.		
The house in the woods is scary.		
You can swim at Al's house.		
Great Gran's house is warm and cosy.		

2 marks

19 Why do you think the poem is called 'House Speak'?
Support your answer with an example from the text.

_____

_____

_____

_____

2 marks

20 Based on the **whole** poem:

a) Which house would you **prefer** to visit and why?

b) Which would be your **least favourite** and why?

Support your answers with evidence from the text.

a) _____

_____

_____

b) _____

_____

_____

2 marks

From *The Traveller's Guide to the Solar System*

by Giles Sparrow

If you want to travel to the Moon and beyond, this is the book for you. Discover the best way to blast off from Earth for a holiday in the Solar System and the most exciting planets to explore when you're there.

Introduction

So you want to take a holiday across the Solar System?

Great idea!

It's an exciting place, and in the modern age of space tourism, lots of people are starting to look beyond Earth for an exotic holiday.

You don't even have to go that far – there are hotels in orbit around Earth, and the Moon is just a short trip away.

If you like, you can get your photograph taken next to the footprints of the first astronauts who landed on the Moon way back in 1969, and return the following day.

If you want to go to the Moon and beyond, you'll need a guidebook like this. We'll show you the highlights of planets and their moons ranging from nearby Venus to faraway Neptune, and take in some other interesting places along the way, including the icy comets and rocky asteroids that follow their own paths around the Sun.

So come with us and enjoy the best the Solar System has to offer. Play hopscotch in the rings of Saturn, go skiing on the Martian ice caps, or explore the mysteries of the Kuiper Belt. There's a lot to see and do – so let's get going!

Getting around the Solar System

In order to reach the other worlds of the Solar System, you'll need to know a little about how things are arranged. The Sun is at the centre of everything, with eight major planets moving around it.

The inner four – Mercury, Venus, Earth and Mars – are rocky and quite small.

The outer four – Jupiter, Saturn, Uranus and Neptune – are much bigger and mostly made of gas and liquid.

Most of the planets have their own moons – smaller worlds that go around them, just like our Moon. In-between and beyond these larger worlds, countless smaller chunks of rock and ice are also going around the Sun.

Every planet has its own orbit – the path it follows because of the pull from the Sun's gravity. Orbits don't have to be perfect circles; they can also be ellipses – stretched ovals that get closer to the Sun at one end than the other.

The closer a planet is to the Sun, the faster it moves around its orbit and the shorter its year. Because of this, the positions of the planets are constantly changing, and every planet is a moving target.

So you'll want to plan your trips around the time when your destination is at its closest to Earth.

From *Three Weird Days and a Meteorite*

by Judy Allen

There was a distant rumbling sound, like far-off thunder. Mike fell flat on his face on the ground. Scott, who'd been walking beside him, was left standing – staring down at him.

"What happened?" said Scott.

"Don't know," said Mike, getting up on to his hands and knees and shaking his head.

"So why did you suddenly dive for cover?"

"I didn't!" said Mike indignantly. He stood up properly and staggered a bit. "Something hit me … on my backpack. I overbalanced and then slipped."

He looked down at himself in disgust. He was covered in wet leaves and so many of them were stuck to his hands that brushing at his clothes didn't help much.

"I'm dirtier than I was at the end of football practice!" he said.

He hauled off his backpack and examined it. It was only about five o'clock, but the November sun sets early and they were between street lamps so it was hard to see. Also, there were so many marks and tiny rips all over the backpack that he couldn't tell if there was a new one or not.

"Can't see where it hit," he said, "but look, it's there!"

Scott looked where he pointed and then bent down, picked up a stone and held it out to Mike on the palm of his hand. "You mean this?" he said.

"Yes," said Mike. "I saw it land."

Instinctively, they both looked around. They were right beside a little row of derelict shops, all boarded up and due to be pulled down. There was nowhere a stone could have fallen from. There was nowhere anyone could have thrown it from.

"There's only one explanation," said Scott, his eyes gleaming. "It must be a meteorite."

"Are you sure?" said Mike. He took the stone from Scott's hand and stared at it. It was small and greyish-black, a little longer than it was wide. The surface was shiny on one side, rough on the other.

Scott waved his arm at the empty, dark sky.

"What else?" he said. "There isn't anything up there. There's no one around; there aren't even any cars. It has to have fallen from space!"

"I'd have thought there'd have been a sonic boom when it came roaring through the air at the speed of light," said Scott wistfully. "Or whatever they do," he added, realising he couldn't claim a huge amount of knowledge about meteorites.

"I think I feel sick," said Mike.

"Why?"

"Because if this is a meteorite, and if it had hit me on the head, I might be dead now."

"There is that," Scott agreed. "But this is amazing. I bet hardly anybody gets hit by a meteorite! Ever! We'll probably have to give it to a museum and we'll probably have to be interviewed on television and stuff. Let's show them at home – who'll be in first, your parents or mine?"

"Dunno," said Mike, stroking the strange stone rather warily. "We can try mine if you like; they're nearer."

When Mike's father got back from work, he wasn't very impressed. "I read somewhere that the chances of being hit by a meteorite are more than a billion to one against," he said.

"That makes it even more important," said Scott.

"Or even less likely," said Mike's father. "More likely a stone got kicked up by a passing car."

"There weren't any passing cars," said both boys together.

"Well then someone threw it."

"There was no one else in the street," said Mike, "honestly," he added.

At that moment, the house seemed to give a slight shudder and the ornaments on the mantelpiece chinked together.

Name: Class: Date:

Questions 1–9 are about *The Traveller's Guide to the Solar System* (pages 54–55).

1 Which statement is the best description of this text?

✓ Tick **one**.

A holiday brochure   ☐

A travel guide to the Moon and beyond   ☐

A description of the Moon   ☐

A travel guide to the Earth   ☐

1 mark

2 *in the modern age of space tourism*

Explain the term *space tourism*.

_____

1 mark

3 **Find** the word *exotic* in the text.

Circle the word that has a similar meaning.

good   relaxing   glamorous   short

1 mark

4 Do you think this is a *real*, current travel guide?
Give a reason for your answer.

_____

_____

1 mark

5 List **two** activities that could be done on Saturn and Mars.

1. _____

2. _____

2 marks

6 Put ticks (✓) in the table to show which of these statements are **fact** and which are **opinion**.

	Fact	Opinion
The sun is at the centre of everything.		
Most planets have their own moons.		
You should travel when the destination is closer.		
You need to learn more about the Solar System before you travel.		

2 marks

7 Why does the text say that *every planet is a moving target*?

Support your answer with reference to the text.

_____

_____

_____

2 marks

8 **Find** and **copy** the description in the text for:

moons _____

orbit _____

_____

2 marks

9 With reference to the **whole** text, give **two** reasons why you think people might like to holiday in the Solar System in the future.

1. _____

_____

2. _____

_____

2 marks

> Questions 10–20 are about
> ***Three Weird Days and a Meteorite*** (pages 56–57).

10 What did the rumbling noise sound like?

_____

1 mark

11 **Find** and **copy** the word that shows Mike was a bit cross at being accused of *diving for cover*.

_____

1 mark

12 Number the sentences below from **1** to **4** to show the order in which events happen.

Mike slipped and landed on the ground. ☐

Mike overbalanced. ☐

Something hit Mike's backpack. ☐

Mike and Scott were walking down the road. ☐

1 mark

13 Do you think it was dark when the incident happened?

Give **two** statements from the text to support your answer.

_____

_____

_____

2 marks

14 Why couldn't Mike tell if his backpack had been damaged?

_____

1 mark

15 *They were right beside a little row of derelict shops*

Explain the word *derelict*.

_____

1 mark

16 Why do you think Mike was stroking the stone *rather warily*?

_____

_____

1 mark

17 Compare Mike and Scott's reactions to the incident.

How did they differ?

Justify your answers with reference to the text.

_____

_____

_____

_____

2 marks

18 How do you think Mike's father felt about the boys' story?

_____

1 mark

19 Complete this table, using evidence from the **whole** text.

Question	Yes, No or Possibly	Evidence
Could the stone have been thrown by someone?		
Could the stone have been kicked up by a passing car?		
Could the stone have fallen from space?		

3 marks

20 How do you think Mike's father's attitude might change at the end of the extract? Give a reason for your answer.

_____

_____

_____

2 marks

Mark scheme for Autumn Half Term Test 1

Qu.	CD	Requirement	Mark
		The Jungle Book	
1	2b	**Award 1 mark** for 2 correct answers: The village children were unkind to Mowgli; Mowgli was learning a new language.	1
2	2b	**Award 1 mark** for each of 2 examples from the text. 1. He didn't understand their games. 2. They called him names and ran away from him.	2
3	2d	**Award 1 mark** for each reference to a human law and appropriate links with his previous life, e.g. he didn't know why they wore so many clothes because he probably didn't wear much when he was living in the jungle; he didn't understand money because he would not have used money when he lived in the jungle.	2
4	2b	**Award 1 mark** for he thought they were not true; they didn't know what they were talking about.	1
5	2a	**Award 1 mark** for to eat grass/plants.	1
6	2d	**Award 1 mark** for any reference to the fact that he felt shocked, frightened or worried and **1 mark** for an explanation, e.g. he knew it meant that Shere Khan had returned.	2
7	2d	**Award 1 mark** for a wolf.	1
8	2b, 2d	**Award 1 mark** for 2–3 correct answers and **2 marks** for 4 correct answers. Shere Khan was dangerous – True; Mowgli's friend was hiding in the bamboo – True; Shere Khan had been away – True; Grey brother would meet Mowgli at nightfall – False.	2
9	2a, 2d	**Award 1 mark** for answers explaining that he was scared or nervous so his heart was beating strongly. Also accept that he had been rushing to get to the tall rock.	1
10	2c, 2d	**Award 1 mark** for a simple answer, e.g. Shere Khan would come for Mowgli. **Award 2 marks** for a more developed answer, using evidence from the text, e.g. Shere Khan and Mowgli would meet and fight. Either Shere Khan or Mowgli would die.	2
		Code Making, Code Breaking	
11	2b	**Award 1 mark** for we all do.	1
12	2a	**Award 1 mark** for each correct answer: cipher – a secret code; encoded – written in a secret code.	1 1
13	2b, 2c	**Award 1 mark** for every 2 correct answers: Greek army – mountaintop bonfires; Native Americans – smoke; Americans fighting the British – lantern flames; The Apache – a code using three plumes of smoke.	2
14	2d	**Award 1 mark** for correct answer (three) and **1 mark** for explanation: one fire could only send a simple message, whereas three fires could give three meanings.	2
15	2b	**Award 1 mark** for each correct answer: one lantern meant the troops were advancing by land; two that they were arriving by sea.	2
16	2a	**Award 1 mark** for *victory*.	1
17	2b, 2c, 2h	**Award 1 mark** for 4–6 correct ticks; **award 2 marks** for all 7 correct ticks; **award 0 marks** if all boxes are ticked: In the home today – a computer password; a mobile phone lock code; a postcode; a secret code. Armies in the past – smoke; a lantern; a secret code.	2
18	2a	**Award 1 mark** for working out what the code means or how it works.	1
19	2b	**Award 1 mark** for to find out the enemy's plan of action.	1
20	2c, 2d	**Award 1 mark** for answers that refer to the text and demonstrate an understanding of the whole text, e.g. Yes – I have a password on my computer to keep it secure.	1
		TOTAL MARKS	30

Mark scheme for Autumn Half Term Test 2

Qu.	CD	Requirement	Mark
		The World's First Women Doctors	
1	2a, 2b	**Award 1 mark** for *unladylike*.	1
2	2b	**Award 1 mark** for each correct name: Elizabeth Garrett Anderson; Elizabeth Blackwell.	2
3	2b	**Award 1 mark** for 1821; Bristol, England.	1
4	2a	**Award 1 mark** for disliked; not popular.	1
5	2b	**Award 1 mark** for each correct point: met interesting people and campaigned against slavery.	2
6	2b	**Award 1 mark** for 4 correct answers: Elizabeth Garrett Anderson spent her childhood in Suffolk – True. Elizabeth Blackwell was born in the USA – False. Elizabeth Blackwell was born before Elizabeth Garrett Anderson – True. Garrett Anderson went to boarding school – True.	1
7	2b, 2d	**Award 1 mark** for what and **1 mark** for why, e.g. *a good education* – so they would be intelligent; have a good start in life; have jobs; contribute to society.	2
8	2c, 2d	**Award 1 mark** for an appropriate suggestion, e.g. trapped; not excited; anxious; worried. **Award 1 mark** for evidence from the text; accept answers that imply that they had been brought up to think for themselves, e.g. they wanted to work for a living; they didn't just want to get married and have families.	2
9	2b, 2d	**Award 1 mark** for every 2 correct answers. Elizabeth Garrett Anderson had brothers and sisters – Fact. Wearing pretty clothes is frivolous – Opinion. Boarding schools provide the best education – Opinion. Girls in the 1800s were expected to get married and have children – Fact.	2
10	2a, 2b	**Award 1 mark** for: to not say what you think or pass judgement	1
		Ruby Redfort: Look into My Eyes	
11	2b	**Award 1 mark** for *on a high stool in front of the bathroom window*.	1
12	2a	**Award 1 mark** for *appeared*.	1
13	2d	**Award 1 mark** for each of 2 reasons, e.g. they were special/private/secret; she had 622 of them; she hid them under floorboards; no one else had read them.	2
14	2b, 2c	**Award 2 marks** for 4 correct answers: 1 = A truck pulled up in Cedarwood Drive. 2 = Ruby drank her banana milk. 3 = Ruby made a note in her notebook. 4 = The telephone rang.	2
15	2c, 2d	**Award 1 mark** for each of 2 reasons, e.g. because she always looked out for things – she had 622 notebooks; reference to her two rules.	2
16	2b	**Award 1 mark** for *ever so slightly different shades of green*.	1
17	2a	**Award 1 mark** for unusual, remarkable, noticeable.	1
18	2g	**Award 1 mark** for each of 2 suitable suggestions, e.g. she answers the phone with a comical made-up name; she also adds a jokey pun.	2
19	2b	**Award 1 mark** for his dad wanted him at home.	1
20	2c, 2d	**Award 1 mark** for each of 2 suitable suggestions using evidence from the text, e.g. determined – she had been keeping the notebooks for nine years; popular – everyone wanted her to like them; nosy/inquisitive – always spying on people; funny – she answered the telephone in a humorous way. Do not accept a physical description.	2
		TOTAL MARKS	30

Mark scheme for Spring Half Term Test 1

Qu.	CD	Requirement	Mark
		Jaws and Claws and Things with Wings	
1	2a	**Award 1 mark** each for study; investigate.	1
2	2a	**Award 1 mark** for 2 words, e.g. *peaceful; smart; quick.*	1
3	2a, 2g	**Award 1 mark** for an answer that shows an emotion, e.g. makes you fall in love with it.	1
4	2b	**Award 1 mark** for a hundred miles.	1
5	2b	**Award 1 mark** for *with a harpoon.* **Award 1 mark** for *meat, oil and bone.*	1 1
6	2b, 2d	**Award 1 mark** for *forests and streams;* or something that suggests freedom or home.	1
7	2d	**Award up to 2 marks** for opinion supported by evidence from the text., e.g. Yes – he was in a sparkling new cage; he was safe; he was being looked after; he was sleeping. No – he was dreaming of freedom; he didn't like being in a cage with people staring and shouting.	2
8	2a	**Award 1 mark** for awaken.	1
9	2d, 2f, 2h	**Award 1 mark** for reference to empathy or sympathy, and **1 mark** for justification from the text, e.g. she is against the hunting of the whales; she feels sorry for the lion asleep in the zoo.	2
		'Step Back, Step Forward'	
10	2b	**Award 1 mark** for *polluting our planet;* also accept *suffocating.*	1
11	2a	**Award 1 mark** for *prior.*	1
12	2a	**Award 1 mark each** for reference to mass produced (e.g. plastic items that were made in large quantities) and disposable (to be thrown away after use).	2
13	2b	Soft drinks came in glass bottles – True. Milk bottles could be reused five times – False. It is still possible to have milk delivered – True. Water bottles were also made of glass – False. **Award 1 mark** for every 2 correct answers.	2
14	2d	**Award 1 mark** for reference to looking for glass drinks bottles lying around, and **1 mark** for reference to obtaining the money back.	2
15	2a	**Award 1 mark** for restricted.	1
16	2b	**Award 1 mark** for four correct answers: sugar, flour, rice, dried fruit.	1
17	2b, 2c, 2d	**Award 1 mark** for 4 correct answers: butter – grocer's; carrots and potatoes – greengrocer's; bread – baker's; beef and lamb – butcher's.	1
18	2d	**Award 1 mark** for reference to the fact that they did not have fridges, and **1 mark** for the result that food would not stay fresh.	2
19	2b, 2d	Plastic is a remarkable product – Opinion. Oil is needed to make plastic– Fact. You are lucky if you still have a milkman– Opinion. People did not used to buy bottled water– Fact. **Award 1 mark** for every 2 correct answers.	2
20	2c, 2d	**Award up to 3 marks** for summarising the fact that people reused and recycled, e.g. • They did not use plastic bags – they shopped with a wicker basket. • They didn't use packaging – food was wrapped in paper, paper bags. • They did not use plastic bottles – milk bottles; drink bottles; water from the tap, etc. Do not award marks for just copying out whole sections of the text.	3
		TOTAL MARKS	**30**

Mark scheme for Spring Half Term Test 2

Qu.	CD	Requirement	Mark
		Michael Rosen: All About Me	
1	2b	**Award 1 mark** for the 11-plus.	1
2	2b	**Award 1 mark** for full of worry.	1
3	2b	**Award 1 mark** each for they did English and Maths tests; they had to move seats.	2
4	2b	**Award 1 mark** for so he could ring the school bell.	1
5	2a	**Award 1 mark** for outcomes.	1
6	2c	**Award 1 mark** for all 4 correct answers. 1 = Michael took the 11-plus exam. 2 = The results arrived. 3 = Friends asked him if he'd passed. 4 = Michael went to grammar school.	1
7	2d	**Award 1 mark** for: before = nervous, *I was so worried that I wouldn't pass.* **Award 1 mark** for: after = relieved, *I did pass though.*	2
8	2a, 2b	**Award 1 mark** for saying *imitating teachers.* **Award 1 mark** for explaining what this means, e.g. pretending to be their teachers – acting and speaking like them.	2
9	2a	**Award 1 mark** for a person's life story, written by themselves.	1
		I Have a Dream	
10	2b	**Award 1 mark** for mother and son.	1
11	2c	**Award 1 mark** for Teresa was confronting Raheem about his attitude.	1
12	2a	**Award 2 marks** for 2 correct adjectives, e.g. shocked, upset, alarmed, appalled.	2
13	2b 2d	a) **Award 1 mark** for an example, e.g. *I don't wanna be a teacher.* b) **Award 1 mark** for the explanation, e.g. to make it sound realistic – it is a chatty conversation between two people who know each other well.	1 1
14	2b, 2d	**Award 1 mark** for every 2 correct answers. Miss Wallace is Raheem's teacher – True. Teresa is a teacher at Raheem's school – True. Raheem got an A star for his work – False. Teresa dreamed of being a teacher when she was young – True.	2
15	2a	**Award 1 mark** for concentrate; work harder; be more serious.	1
16	2d 2b	**Award 1 mark** for how he feels, e.g. not at all happy; embarrassed. **Award 1 mark** for anything from the text that shows he is not happy, *e.g. Are you serious? You can't do that! But ... what about me? This is so unfair!*	1 1
17	2d	**Award 1 mark** for his mother is much harder on him than she would be on them.	1
18	2b, 2d	Martin Luther King was shot dead – Fact. It is a good thing to be rich and famous – Opinion. Martin Luther King helped to change the lives of black people – Fact. It is boring learning about Martin Luther King – Opinion. **Award 2 marks** for every 2 correct answers.	2
19	2c, 2d	**Award 1 mark** for cross with Raheem; frustrated; annoyed, disappointed, etc. **Award 1 mark** for any appropriate reference to the text, e.g. *You can go to your room. Do you even care about your future?*	2
20	2d	Yes. **Award 1 mark** for each quotation from the text, e.g. *I'm fed up of hearing about that guy; Here we go again.*	2
		TOTAL MARKS	**30**

Mark scheme for Summer Half Term Test 1

Qu.	CD	Requirement	Mark
		The Boswall Kidnapping	
1	2b	**Award 1 mark** for *like school trousers; sensible.*	1
2	2b	**Award 1 mark** for by the way he was standing: head down and saggy shoulders.	1
3	2b, 2f	**Award 2 marks** for 2 references that show strange behaviour, e.g. • looking behind him • wandering around the kitchen department • looking at the floor.	2
4	2d	**Award 1 mark** for because he was nervous; it was a shock; he was frightened.	1
5	2b	**Award 1 mark** for *confused* and **1 mark** for *embarrassed.*	2
6	2b	**Award 1 mark** for he had lost his mum.	1
7	2b	**Award 1 mark** for *mean* – do not accept alternatives. **Award 1 mark** for explanations that refer to the text, e.g. the boy *was only young*, *a bit wimpy*; *didn't know his way around.*	2
8	2b	**Award 1 mark** for 4 correct answers: 1 = Alex was shopping with his father. 2 = The boy was crying on the escalator. 3 = The boy entered the furniture department. 4 = Alex followed him into the kitchen department.	1
9	2c	**Award 2 marks** for 2 pieces of evidence taken from the whole text, e.g. young, wimpy, wearing school trousers, tee-shirt untucked; floppy blond fringe.	2
10	2e	**Award 1 mark** for any plausible prediction based on the clues in the title or the text, e.g. • The boy might get kidnapped. • The mum might have been kidnapped so they have to get her back. • Alex might help the boy to find his mum.	1
		'House Speak'	
11	2c	**Award 1 mark** for: This poem describes a number of different houses.	1
12	2h, 2f	**Award 1 mark** for how the houses compare: the old house is warm and comfortable; the new house is the opposite – it's very new and cold. Also accept modern or newly decorated.	1
		Award 1 mark for the narrator prefers the old one.	1
13	2a	**Award 1 mark** for unwelcoming.	1
14	2d, 2g	**Award 1 mark** for reference to expression, e.g. to stress it when you are reading it; or for the reason behind it, e.g. because it is unusual to have two staircases – the narrator can't believe it!	1
15	2d	**Award 1 mark** for a flat / tower block. **Award 1 mark** for any reference to the text – *way up high*; *calls to you from the clouds*; *press the button* – on the lift.	2
16	2b, 2d	**Award 1 mark** for mentioning that ruined means spoiled and **1 mark** for the narrator thinks it is a wonderful place to play.	2
17	2b	**Award 1 mark** for three suggestions: old; grey on top; stoops, leans; sighs; tired eyes.	1

Qu.	CD	Requirement	Mark
18	2b, 2d	**Award 1 mark** for every 2 correct answers. You can see for miles from Leah's house – True. The house in the woods is scary – False. You can swim at Al's house – True. Great Gran's house is warm and cosy – True.	2
19	2d, 2f	**Award 1 mark** for the reason, e.g. because the houses seem to speak to you. They have personalities and reflect their owners. **Award 1 mark** for the evidence, e.g. the old house said 'Come in', but the new one said 'Keep out'.	2
20	2c, 2d, 2h	**Award 1 mark** for each appropriate answer supported by reference to the houses in the poem, e.g. prefer Leah's house because I would like to go up in the lift and look out over the city.	2
		TOTAL MARKS	30

Mark scheme for Summer Half Term Test 2

Qu.	CD	Requirement	Mark
		The Traveller's Guide to the Solar System	
1	2c	**Award 1 mark** for A travel guide to the Moon and beyond.	1
2	2a	**Award 1 mark** for holiday travel in space.	1
3	2a	**Award 1 mark** for glamorous.	1
4	2d	**Award 1 mark** for No – because we cannot currently travel through space to all the other planets, or get to the Moon and back in two days.	1
5	2b	**Award 1 mark** for *hopscotch* and **1 mark** for *skiing*.	2
6	2d	**Award 1 mark** for every 2 correct answers. The sun is at the centre of everything – Fact; Most planets have their own moon – Fact; You should travel when the destination is closer – Opinion; You need to learn more about the Solar System before you travel – Opinion.	2
7	2b, 2d	**Award 1 mark** for it is difficult to keep up with them or land on them. **Award 1 mark** for references to the fact that they are always moving; planets have their own orbit; they move around the sun; orbits aren't perfect circles; they move faster at times.	1 1
8	2a	**Award 1 mark** for: moons – *smaller worlds that go around them.* **Award 1 mark** for: orbit – *the path it follows because of the pull from the Sun's gravity.*	1 1
9	2b, 2e	**Award 1 mark** for each reason that is based on evidence from the text, e.g. to see footprints on the Moon; interesting places; there's a lot to see.	2
		Three Weird Days and a Meteorite	
10	2b	**Award 1 mark** for *far-off thunder.*	1
11	2a	**Award 1 mark** for *indignantly.*	1
12	2d	**Award 1 mark** for 4 correct answers. 1 = Mike and Scott were walking down the road. 2 = Something hit Mike's backpack. 3 = Mike overbalanced. 4 = Mike slipped and landed on the ground.	1
13	2d	Yes. **Award 1 mark** for each of 2 correct statements from the text, e.g. it was 5 o'clock in November; sun sets early; they were between street lamps so it was hard to see.	2
14	2b	**Award 1 mark** for it had so many marks and rips on it already.	1
15	2a	**Award 1 mark** for e.g. abandoned; run-down; empty; dilapidated.	1
16	2a, 2d, 2f	**Award 1 mark** for understanding of the word *warily* with any reference to the text that would lead to Mike's caution, e.g. because he was nervous after the incident; because it might have come from space; because he could have been killed.	1
17	2d, 2h	Mike – nervous; shocked; confused; felt sick; realised he could have been killed. Scott – excited; amazed; looking forward to the fame and attention.	2
18	2d	**Award 1 mark** for he didn't believe them – he was sceptical; unimpressed.	1
19	2b, 2d	**Award 1 mark** for each correct answer with appropriate evidence from the text. No – there was no one around; No – there were no cars; Possibly – e.g. it must have fallen from somewhere; it looked unusual – shiny on one side, rough on the other.	3
20	2d, 2h	**Award 1 mark** for the change in attitude and **1 mark** for the evidence, e.g. he might start to believe that something strange is going on because of the shudder and the ornaments on the mantelpiece chinked together.	2
		TOTAL MARKS	30

Name:	Class:

Year 5 Reading Comprehension Record Sheet

Tests	Mark	Total marks	Key skills to target
Autumn Half Term Test 1			
Autumn Half Term Test 2			
Spring Half Term Test 1			
Spring Half Term Test 2			
Summer Half Term Test 1			
Summer Half Term Test 2			